Tyneside

Building sl
work calli
beer when
on every

At the turn of the century 1000 public houses in the Tyneside area. Some of the pubs were private houses which had been converted by an enterprising Geordie who may have even brewed the beer on the premises. Many pubs were designed by local architects however and were superb examples of the very best architectural style of the time. The funding for the building of these pubs was often provided by the Breweries such as Robert Deuchar Ltd, James Deuchar Ltd, John Rowell and Son Ltd, Matthew Wood and Son Ltd and of course Newcastle Breweries Ltd. In the 1950's many of the breweries were either merging or being taken over by larger companies. The whole pub scene took on a major rationalization in the 1960's resulting in the closing and eventual demolition of dozens of fine Tyneside pubs such as the Trafalgar shown opposite.

Haymarket Hotel and Plough Hotel, Haymarket 1960's Both pubs were handy for a swift half before meeting the girlfriend and taking her to the Haymarket Cinema next door. If you were a really big spender, you could buy her a Barbecue Express chicken supper after the film.

King's Head, Blackett Street/Percy Street 1950's   The King's Head was a James Deuchar's house and the beer was delivered by boat from Deuchar's Brewery in Montrose. To the right of the pub is Bower's shop. Ronnie Bower opened Newcastle's first 24 hour fast-food restaurant on Neville Street in the 1960's.

Chancellor's Head, Newgate Street Newcastle 1966 The Chancellor's Head stood at No 118 Newgate Street opposite St Andrew's Church. The pub was closed in February 1971 and eventually was demolished along with many other fine pubs in order to build Eldon Square

Lion and Lamb, Newgate Street Newcastle 1966   A little further along Newgate Street at No 134 was the Lion and Lamb, which was listed in directories dated 1788. Birrell's sweet shop is seen to the left.

Leazes Tavern, Crescent Place Newcastle 1966 The Leazes Tavern stood on the corner of Leazes Lane and Crescent Place close to Leazes Park. It was also close to St James's football ground and was probably a favourite haunt of Newcastle United supporters. It was closed in 1967.

Carlisle, Westgate Road Newcastle 1966 Home to motorbike showrooms, sleazy bookshops, and private cinema clubs, Westgate Road used to have over 30 pubs. Among the other pubs on Westgate Road which went for a Burton were; Marquis of Blandford, William IV, North-Eastern, Express, and the Goat.

Wellington Inn, Barrack Road Newcastle 1920 The Wellington Inn stood at the corner of Barrack Road and Wellington Street. The pub later became the Novocastrian Club which was frequented by musicians and music-hall artists. They didn't have to go far for supplies of beer as Newcastle Breweries were just yards away.

Lambert's Leap, Sandyford Road Newcastle 1966 In 1795 Cuthbert Lambert, the son of a famous Newcastle physician, was riding along Sandyford Road when his horse bolted and jumped the parapet of a bridge and into the ravine below making an enormous leap. Lambert's fall was broken by the protruding branch of an old ash tree, but the horse was killed. The event caused a sensation and became known as Lambert's Leap giving its name to the pub. The pub was demolished in 1972.

Blyth and Tyne, New Bridge Street Newcastle 1966 The Blyth and Tyne was named after the Blyth and Tyne railway which terminated at New Bridge Street station. To the right of the pub is Tulip's newsagent shop and further right are the Oxford Salerooms.

New Railway, Carliol Place Newcastle 1966   Formerly the Goods Station Inn, built in 1890, the New Railway was demolished in the 1970's to build the Central Motorway East. The tall building behind is Carliol House which was built on the site of the town jail.

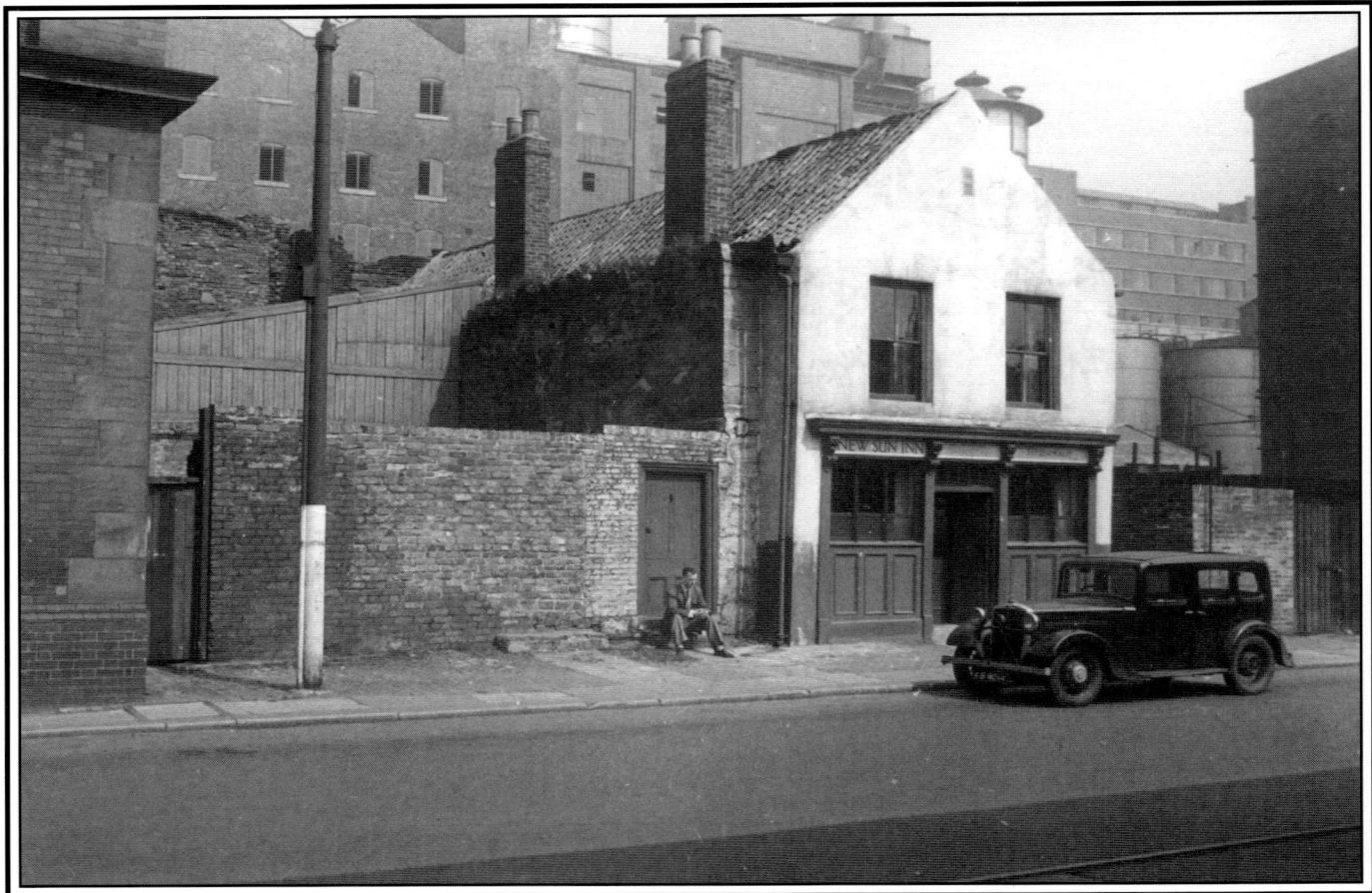

New Sun Inn, Quayside 1955 This very old pub was listed in directories dated 1788. To the left is the Co-operative Wholesale Society warehouse which has been renovated and is to be part of the new Sandgate development near the Quayside. The buildings behind the pub are Thomas Hedley's soap factories.

**Golden Lion, Tyne Street
(off City Road) Newcastle 1966**
The Golden Lion was a Duncan and Daglish owned pub which stood on Tyne Street. Opposite the pub was the Tynearc Welding Co. and in the distance is St Ann's Row.

Princess Royal, Jesmond Vale 1914 The kids are playing in the Ouse Burn, a tributary of the River Tyne. A few hundred yards further upstream are the beautiful parklands of Jesmond Dene; a gift to the City of Newcastle upon Tyne by Lord Armstrong in 1883.

Duke of York, Back Maling Street, St Lawrence 1920 Formerly the Dog Inn , it was known locally as Jocker Wood's. The pub was a free house and was in a poor state of repair when in the late 1930's the building collapsed in a strong gust of wind with some of the regulars still drinking inside. The pub closed in 1944.

Bay Horse, Byker Bank 1966

The Bay Horse originally sold George Younger's ales, then moved over to Flower's ales. Whitbread bought the pub in the 1960's and Nimmo's ales were then sold. Other bygone boozers on Byker Bank were Half Moon, Byker Tavern, and New Hawk nicknamed Dyer Browns.

Addison, Tynemouth Road Heaton 1966 Originally the Addison was a free house owned by Tommy Shaw. He sold the pub to James Deuchar which eventually was bought up by Scottish and Newcastle Breweries.

Neptune, Fisher Street Walker 1966   This pub took its name from Swan Hunter's Neptune Yard which sadly is no longer building ships. The Neptune Hotel was where the more wealthy ships' captains would lodge while their ships were being refitted. The pub was originally run by a local brewery called W B Reid & Co.

Cumberland Arms, Church Street Walker 1966 The Cumberland Arms used to be run by a man called Duffy whose brother managed the Plough on Byker Bank. Further along Church Street was the Fountain; another pub to succumb to the bulldozer.

Railway Inn, High Street Wallsend 1915 The railways made such an impact on Victorian Tynesiders that they named pubs after them. Opposite the Railway Inn was the Ship Hotel which also met its demise.